M000306895

Nurturing Your Self While Caring for Another

Rose Kaszycki
and
Juanita Liepelt, SFO

Nurturing Your Self While Caring for Another. Copyright © 2007
Rose Kaszycki and Juanita Liepelt, SFO. Printed and bound in the
United States of America. All rights reserved. No part of this book
may be reproduced or transmitted in any form or by any means,
electronic or mechanical, including photocopying, recording, or
by an information storage and retrieval system without permission
in writing from the publisher, except by a reviewer who may
quote brief passages in a review. Published by RealityIs Books,
an imprint of RealityIsBooks.com, Inc., 309 East Rand Road,
Unit 313, Arlington Heights, IL 60004. Tel: 866-534-3366, Email:
publish@RealityIsBooks.com.

Although the author and publisher have made every effort to
ensure the accuracy and completeness of information contained
in this book, no responsibility is assumed for errors, inaccuracies,
omissions, or any inconsistency herein. Any slights of people,
places, or organizations are unintentional.

First printing 2007
EAN: 978-0-9791317-4-5.
ISBN: 0-9791317-4-X

ATTENTION Corporations, Universities, Colleges, and
Professional Organizations: Quantity discounts are available on
bulk purchases of this book for educational, gift purposes, or as
premiums. Special books or book excerpts can also be created to
fit specific needs. For information, please contact RealityIs Books,
an imprint of RealityIsBooks.com, Inc., 309 East Rand Road,
Unit 313, Arlington Heights, IL 60004. Tel: 866-534-3366, Email:
publish@RealityIsBooks.com.

To our parents, Stanley and Sylvia Kotlinski, who continued to teach us how to live by their examples, even when their own health was declining.

The reflections shared in this book are written from our hearts to yours, with the hope that you will find the hope and courage, sprinkled with a smile and sense of humor, to carry on through what can be a very difficult time. The books from which the quotations have been taken are highly recommended reading.

Nurturing Your Self While Caring for Another

"If you don't love yourself, you cannot love someone else. If you cannot accept yourself, if you cannot treat yourself with kindness, you cannot do this for another person."

Anger: Wisdom for Cooling the Flame
Thich Nhat Hanh

THOUGHT FOR THE DAY

It almost sounds selfish to think of loving yourself when a family member needs your attention. I need to remember that caring for myself is also an act of kindness toward another.

- 1 -

REFLECTION

At the beginning of an airline flight, the attendants tell the passengers that in the event of an emergency, the passengers should put on their own oxygen mask first, before attempting to help anyone else. This makes perfect sense when we think of it, but how many of us actually do this? Instead, we put ourselves last, thinking it is the noble thing to do, and often as a result our own health can begin to deteriorate while caring for a loved one.

- 2 -

"Spoil yourself with gifts of time—time to know yourself better and time to love and appreciate those who are a part of your life."

Why People Don't Heal and How They Can
Caroline Myss, Ph.D.

THOUGHT FOR THE DAY

Spending time with family members can be the most valuable gift you can give, but learning to enjoy spending time alone with your Self will have benefits beyond belief!

- 2 -

REFLECTION

Sometimes when we have a lot of stress and chaos in our lives and it feels as if life is spinning out of control in a downward spiral, the first thing we want to do is pick up the phone and talk to someone about it. There's a feeling of relief in discussing the stressful situation with someone, and often the last thing we want to do is spend quiet time with ourselves. There certainly is a time to connect with another person; however, the truth is that spending quiet time emptying our minds of the stress is actually healthier than *continually* talking about it. This does not mean that stress should be ignored; however, going *over* and *over* the situation only gives it more power and the effects of the stress tend to stay with us longer.

- 3 -

"Imagine trying to hurry nature up by tugging at an emerging tomato plant—you're as natural as that plant, so let yourself be at peace with the perfection of nature's plan."

Inspiration: Your Ultimate Calling
Wayne W. Dyer, Ph.D.

THOUGHT FOR THE DAY

This reminds me that I must have patience with myself and with those around me. God's plan unfolds one day at a time, just as the petals of a rose open slowly one day at a time. Neither can be hurried.

REFLECTION

It's easier for me to have patience with someone else, especially someone who is sick, than to have patience with myself. It has been very kindly pointed out to me that when I become impatient with myself, it's because I allow my ego to run the show. I realize how true that is, since the underlying feeling I have when I become impatient with myself is that I think I should be doing better than I am. I need to keep this in mind, and show the same compassion and understanding to myself as I do for others.

- 4 -

"Every free choice involves suffering. To say yes to love involves saying no to something else. One cannot both help the homeless man who has had a seizure on the street where one is walking and get to the grocery store before it closes. One cannot be charitable to anyone without giving something— time, effort, money, or something else."

The Healer's Calling:
A Spirituality for Physicians and Other Health Care
Professionals
Daniel P. Sulmasy, O.F.M., M.D.

THOUGHT FOR THE DAY

I have to come to terms with the fact that the time I spend being a caregiver takes time away from something else. If I led a busy life before becoming a caregiver, some parts of that life will have to change dramatically because I will spend that time caring for someone rather than being involved in life as usual.

- 4 -

REFLECTION

Rose was living fifty miles away from her parents
when her Dad was diagnosed with lung cancer.
She took a leave of absence from her job and
rented an apartment nearby to help look after her
parents. During the week, Rose's main focus was
her parents; she was wife and mother on weekends
when she drove back home, and Juanita would be
with their parents. During this time, Juanita was
in graduate school two evenings a week and had a
full time job. She would go straight to her parents'
home after work or school and stay with them until
they were settled in for the night. As her parents'
health declined, she stayed with them during the
night and left for work from their home. Rose
would come in the morning and stay the day.

"Even the slightest irritation is significant
and needs to be acknowledged and looked at;
otherwise, there will be a cumulative build-up of
unobserved reactions."

The Power of Now
Eckhart Tolle

THOUGHT FOR THE DAY

Even the slightest irritation can grow to be a
crippling resentment if it isn't acknowledged and
examined so that it can be dissolved.

- 5 -

REFLECTION

When we are not mindful of our feelings and thoughts, we can allow irritations to take root and become resentments. Over time, learning the practice of mindfulness, rather than going through life on automatic pilot, helps to eliminate stress from our lives.

- 6 -

"Many new fears emerge following the diagnosis of an illness, or when you encounter a setback or tragedy in your life. You need to be patient with yourself."

Why People Don't Heal and How They Can
Caroline Myss, Ph.D.

THOUGHT FOR THE DAY

Being patient with ourselves is most often the last of our concerns, the first of course being our loved one who is sick. We need to remember that we can only work within our human limitations, and that our faith in God is all we can truly rely on.

- 6 -

REFLECTION

I remember becoming numb when Dad told me that he went to his primary care physician, and that she had given him a referral to see an oncologist. Dad never had much use for such fancy words, and he asked me if I ever heard of that word, "oncologist." With a lump in my throat and fighting to hold back tears, I explained what I could, adding that I was sure his doctor wanted to rule out the most serious possibilities first. With all my heart, I wanted to make things better for my Dad, who was always and still is my hero. All I could do, however, is ask my Dad if I could come with him and Mom to his appointment with the oncologist.

- 7 -

"Look around you now and notice what you are grateful for. You may see large things or small ones—a pattern of light on the wall, a person or pet, a concept, a state of being, a world—whatever."

A Passion for the Possible
Jean Houston

THOUGHT FOR THE DAY

It's a good idea to be mindful of the many little things we have to be grateful for, and to intentionally recall these things—especially at the end of day. Over time, they blend together and give us a good foundation for a positive outlook on life.

- 7 -

REFLECTION

Developing an attitude of gratitude can be difficult, and it's not something that happens quickly. The seeds of gratitude within us need to be watered daily. It takes a lot of work and its results are not quickly evident. If we practice gratitude on a daily basis, one day we will be surprised at how easily we can deal with a situation that would have made us angry or resentful. The results are well worth the work!

- 8 -

"One word can give comfort and confidence, destroy doubt, help someone avoid a mistake, reconcile a conflict, or open the door to liberation."

Peace is Every Step:
The Path of Mindfulness in Everyday Life
Thich Nhat Hanh

THOUGHT FOR THE DAY

A word or an unspoken attitude can make so much difference to someone, especially someone who is sick and has limited involvement with life outside the home.

- 8 -

REFLECTION

Dad was a steelworker and had significant hearing loss because of the noise he experienced on a daily basis. He always told his doctors about his diminished hearing at the beginning of an appointment so that they would be sure he understood everything that was said. When we went in to meet with Dad's first oncologist, Dad asked the doctor a question about something that he had just said. The doctor, with all the compassion of a jackhammer, shot an impatient glance at me and said, "Will you tell him what I just said?" Tears filled my eyes when I saw the hurt look on Dad's face. Dad had asked his question with all the respect he could summon up, even though he was sick and worried not only about himself but his wife, our Mom. Needless to say, we quickly found a new oncologist for Dad. He was a kind man who stood right next to Dad and put his arm around Dad's shoulder when he spoke to him.

" 'Two people can ride the same roller coaster,'
I pointed out. 'One is terrified, and his body is
flooded with stress hormones, causing his immune
response to plummet. The other loves roller
coasters, and he produces a flood of chemicals, such
as interferon and interleukin, that strengthen his
immune system. Same input, opposite results, all
because of a different point of view.' "

Unconditional Life:
Mastering the Forces that Shape Personal Reality
Deepak Chopra, M.D.

THOUGHT FOR THE DAY

The truth of the matter is that, although we may
have no control over what happens to us, we do
have control over our response to the situation.

- 9 -

REFLECTION

Ever since I became aware of the stress hormone, cortisol, and its negative effects on the body's immune system, I have worked very hard not to allow stress to be a part of my life. Learning to remain calm in spite of the chaos was no small task for someone who once suffered stress induced migraines.

- *10* -

"We do not simply listen in order to know what to say. If that were so, then speaking would be more important than listening. To give one's whole attention to another is itself a gracious act."

All Our Losses, All Our Griefs
Kenneth R. Mitchell and Herbert Anderson

THOUGHT FOR THE DAY

Help me to be aware that the person I am caring for has the need to be heard. Help me to have patience and tolerance even though I might be hearing the same stories again and again.

- 10 -

REFLECTION

Mom would sit in the waiting room with us when we took Dad for his radiation treatments, and ask us again and again "Why are we here?" Either Dad or one of us would patiently tell her. After Dad went in for the treatment, Mom would repeatedly tell us that she wished she could have gone in with Dad, and that she hoped Dad would remember to tell her everything the doctor said. We repeatedly told Mom that Dad only went in for the radiation treatment, and that there was no doctor appointment. We assured her that she would be able to go in with Dad and us when he met with the doctor. When the person we are caring for has been diagnosed with dementia, we need to have patience and compassion because their need to be heard is not diminished even though their ability to function is diminished.

- *11* -

"We have walked through different gardens and knelt at different graves. Your sad memories make you heartweary or heartsick, while I am perfectly immune to them. Likewise, the joyful images that gladden our hearts may closely resemble each other, but your memories have a personal flavor that I cannot taste."

Unconditional Life:
Mastering the Forces that Shape Personal Reality
Deepak Chopra, M.D.

THOUGHT FOR THE DAY

I must remember never to tell someone "I know exactly how you feel." Even though our experiences may be very similar, there are always so many different aspects to a situation, that to tell someone I know how he or she feels may even be disrespectful to their pain.

- *11* -

REFLECTION

Even among family members experiencing the same loss, responses to a situation may be as different as night and day. Relationships differ and levels of communication differ. I need to keep this in mind always so that I can have compassion even though I may not thoroughly understand the situation.

- *12* -

"You may feel that you should keep feelings of sadness and grief to yourself and not burden others with your troubles. However, sharing these feelings can be comforting and can give you the strength you need to continue to care for a declining person."

The 36-Hour Day
Nancy L. Mace, M.A.
Peter V. Rabins, M.D., M.P.H

THOUGHT FOR THE DAY

Feelings of grief and sadness can weigh you down, and it can feel almost like having a ton of bricks on your chest. Sharing those feelings with others, perhaps in a support group or with a caring physician, can help ease the stress of a situation.

- *12* -

REFLECTION

Rose and Juanita talked on the phone every evening about how Dad was feeling that day and to try to figure out what might be going on with their Mom. Was it depression because her husband of nearly sixty years was diagnosed with cancer? Dad would not allow us to bring up Mom's behavior to their doctor. However, a short time after Dad passed away, Rose and Juanita decided to talk with Mom's primary care doctor because Mom's safety was beginning to be a real concern. Dr. Dorothy met with them, tested Mom, then held a conference call with them that lasted nearly four hours so that she could explain the results of the test and answer their questions. If only there were more Dr. Dorothys in this world!

- *13* -

"Remind yourself that acceptance of the present moment has nothing to do with resignation in the face of what is happening. It simply means a clear acknowledgment that *what is happening is happening.*"

Wherever You Go, There You Are
Jon Kabat-Zinn

THOUGHT FOR THE DAY

There's an old saying that you can't fix something unless you know it's broken. I need to remember this and ask for help on a daily basis to see things as they are and not as I wish they were.

- *13* -

REFLECTION

I fought the idea of acceptance for a long time because I thought it meant that I was OK with the situation at hand. How far from the truth! I realize now that acceptance of a situation *as it is* actually makes me more capable of changing the situation because I know exactly what I am dealing with.

- 14 -

"When you are full of problems, there is no room for anything new to enter, no room for a solution. So whenever you can, make some room, create some space, so that you find the life underneath your life situation."

The Power of Now
Eckhart Tolle

THOUGHT FOR THE DAY

A vessel cannot be filled with two things at the same time. I need to remember that in order to achieve peace and calm in my life, I have to stop making problems out of situations in my life.

- *14* -

REFLECTION

I've learned that a problem is simply a situation which is not turning out the way I want it to turn out. Looking back, I see that many situations I thought of as problems worked themselves out better than I could have imagined, and I can see that they were blessings in disguise. I have to let go of the fear of situations I cannot control and remember the times that my faith has been my only true source of comfort.

- 15 -

"When we are confronted with anguish, pain or illness—when we feel as if we *must* pray—we are not likely to deliberate about whether or not we shall pursue a specific or nonspecific approach, or whether sound or silence is more appropriate. In the immediacy of the moment, we simply *pray*."

Healing Words:
The Power of Prayer and the Practice of Medicine
Larry Dossey, M.D.

THOUGHT FOR THE DAY

Prayer is a source of comfort because it reminds us that there is a higher power watching out for us. It makes no difference what words or name we give to that higher power. What makes a difference is the depth of our faith.

- *15* -

REFLECTION

When Dad was admitted to the hospital because of an irreparable bleeding ulcer, and the staff talked to us about end of life decisions, we were all thrown off balance emotionally. We had been told that Dad's chemotherapy was working, and no one suspected a bleeding ulcer until it was too large to cauterize, and Dad's weakened condition would not allow surgery. All we could do was wait and pray for a merciful end. With all the resources available to us, when the machines told us that the end was near and the medical staff ushered us out of the room, all I could do is take Mom into the hall, hug her, and pray the Our Father with her. Once, twice, three times over, and then again.

- *16* -

"Looking back, I can see that the times of adversity have each taught me something which has given my life extra quality and depth, even though, at the time, I did not always welcome these challenges."

The Feeling Buddha:
A Buddhist Psychology of Character, Adversity and Passion
David Brazier

THOUGHT FOR THE DAY

It's the most difficult times in life that help us to grow spiritually. Many of the great mystics in history have experienced what they referred to as dark nights of the soul. As hard as it is, help me to accept these challenges and to see them as opportunities for spiritual growth.

- *16* -

REFLECTION

When we look back on the challenging situations of the past, it's not that difficult to see the lessons we learned from them. What's difficult is staying in the moment, and treating these challenges as the gifts they are, knowing that somehow, at some time in the future, we will appreciate the lessons learned.

- 17 -

"As you help a forgetful person enjoy the world around him, you may experience a renewed delight in sharing little things—playing with a puppy or enjoying flowers. You may discover a new faith in yourself, in others, or in God."

The 36-Hour Day
Nancy L. Mace, M.A.
Peter V. Rabins, M.D., M.P.H

THOUGHT FOR THE DAY

Help me to remember that as a person's health declines, his or her ability to do many things also declines. I need to remember that it's the little things that I take for granted in everyday life that can be enjoyed the most by someone who is homebound.

- *17* -

REFLECTION

After Dad passed away, and before Mom was diagnosed with Alzheimer's Disease, I would often pick up Mom after work and we would go out for supper, often trying a new restaurant just to have a break in her routine. Afterwards, we would go for a drive and see what we could see. Mom especially liked to drive through downtown Chicago, pointing out places that she recognized. Her face glowed as she told me stories about when she and Dad took the streetcar downtown when they were dating. Seeing the sights through her eyes helped me see downtown Chicago in a new way, even though I worked there everyday.

- 18 -

"Try going out into the woods or sitting very near the ocean's waves. Look up at the bright stars at night; open your mind's inner ear and listen to the lovely song of silence. Here is the joy of contemplative sweetness. Follow this bliss."

Awakening The Buddha Within:
Tibetan Wisdom for the Western World
Lama Surya Das

THOUGHT FOR THE DAY:

There is no better method of relaxation for me than simply being in nature, listening to the waves upon the shore, the rustle of the leaves, and meditating upon the majesty of trees. Take some time today, however briefly, to lose your self in nature, whether it's walking down a path or looking at the tops of trees from your window.

- *18* -

REFLECTION:

When I see the tiny leaves of the crocus coming out of the hard frozen ground in the spring, I cannot help but marvel at the wonder of it all, how these tiny soft leaves make their way through the nearly frozen soil! When I see the tiny leaves held onto the branches of the trees throughout even the most violent storms, I thank God for such reminders of the goodness of the universe, and know beyond a shadow of a doubt that I, too, will be taken care of, even through the most difficult storms of life.

- *19* -

"Situations arise in everyone's life that are difficult to acknowledge—for example, a child on drugs or a marriage that is in great difficulty. Acknowledging the situation, which means discussing it, makes it real in such a way that one can no longer deny the problem."

The Creation of Health:
The Emotional, Psychological and Spiritual Responses That
Promote Health and Healing
Caroline Myss, Ph.D.
Norman Shealy, M.D., Ph.D.

THOUGHT FOR THE DAY

One of the most difficult things to cope with is the reality that a loved one has an incurable disease. I pray for the courage to look at the situation as it is, not as I wish it was, so that I can make decisions that are in the best interest of my loved one.

- *19* -

REFLECTION

I can still remember when Mom's primary care doctor told us that she suspected a diagnosis of Alzheimer's Disease. The kind doctor told us that Alzheimer's could only be definitely diagnosed with an autopsy, and that all we could do at this time was to eliminate all other possible reasons for Mom's behavior. It's not that we wanted to put a label on Mom, it was just that we believed if we had a name, we would be more likely to provide proper care for Mom. We want to make a point of stressing the importance of ruling out other possible reasons for dementia, since it could be the symptom of an illness requiring specific care.

- 20 -

"It is still sometimes easier for me to lose myself in work or reading than to face painful feelings that are tapping on my shoulder, trying to give me a message about my past and its relation to present behaviors and relationships."

Guilt is the Teacher, Love is the Lesson
Joan Borysenko, Ph.D.

THOUGHT FOR THE DAY

I need to be mindful of what's really going on with me. Am I throwing myself into my work in order to avoid looking at a situation, or does the work truly require so much of my attention?

- 20 -

REFLECTION

If my mind is kept busy by focusing on a project or the plot of a book, there isn't room to think about what's going on in my life. Sometimes I desperately need to empty my mind of the stress of the day, even though I know that sooner or later I have to face reality. I need to remember that its OK to take these breaks as long as I don't use them to avoid reality.

- 21 -

"Not everyone has the capability to be a full-time caregiver .... Sometimes the most responsible thing you can do is to recognize that someone else should provide the day-to-day physical care."

The 36-Hour Day
Nancy L. Mace, M.A.
Peter V. Rabins, M.D., M.P.H

THOUGHT FOR THE DAY

Making the decision to put the care of your loved one in the hands of another brings up a flood of so many emotions that it is almost impossible to think clearly at first. Know that this is normal and that it will pass.

- *21* -

REFLECTION

We did our best to care for Mom by ourselves at her home, but after a while it became evident that we were not capable of being Mom's full time caregivers. One of us felt it would be best to have Mom stay at her home and have caregivers come in, and one of us felt it would be better for Mom if we found a residence for her. There were pros and cons to each situation, and each of us knew people who had made this decision or that one. The only thing we agreed on was that we wanted what was best for Mom. Our respect for each other and our willingness to really listen to the other's opinion enabled us to have open and honest discussions. After much deliberation, we came to the decision to begin interviewing residences for Mom.

For us, and for Mom, the best was a residence for memory loss patients, which is part of a nursing center. Mom is happy, and we are grateful knowing that we made the right decision for her.

"For what you embrace on the conscious level, if it does not correspond to who you are on the unconscious level, it is really an acting out of what you think others expect of you or what you expect of yourself."

The Way of St. Francis:
The Challenge of Franciscan Spirituality for Everyone
Murray Bodo, O.F.M.

THOUGHT FOR THE DAY

Shakespeare wrote "to thine own self be true." It's important to remember that our actions, thoughts, and words need to be a reflection of what is in our hearts.

- 22 -

REFLECTION

It's so easy to reflect the expectations of others, especially in a stressful situation where a family member requires a caregiver. No one wants to add to the stress by being confrontational, and sometimes a person might go along with a plan just to keep the peace. We have to have the courage to follow our hearts rather than the expectations of others. I know today that what I think, what I do, and what I say need to be in alignment with each other. When they are not, I feel out-of-sorts and anxious.

- 23 -

"Wise lamas encouraged me to meditate on the difficulties themselves—just to be present with the difficulty, as it were, instead of trying to get over it as quickly as possible. To face the doubt rather than try to avoid or suppress it. In this process I learned something that millions of seekers had also learned before me and millions will after me: You have to go through the darkness to truly know the light."

Awakening The Buddha Within:
Tibetan Wisdom for the Western World
Lama Surya Das

THOUGHT FOR THE DAY

I need to remember that the only way I can get through a tough situation is by wholeheartedly acknowledging it. While avoiding it or refusing to accept it may temporarily put it off, chances are that it won't go away and might even get worse.

- 23 -

REFLECTION

It was an unspoken fact that we would care for our parents as they advanced in age, and one of the most difficult things either of us has had to do is accept the fact that Mom required care beyond what we could give her. We realize now that by keeping Mom at home, we would be satisfying our needs and not hers. When we finally accepted the reality and acknowledged the need to find a residence for Mom, we hit another brick wall: we had no idea what criteria to use when interviewing residences. A friend of Juanita's from church had a friend who had professional experience in this area, and he provided the direction we needed to chose a wonderful residence for Mom. Mom now eats well and, within her limitations, exercises and takes part in various activities. We celebrated Mom's 91st birthday on the Fourth of July, 2007!

- 24 -

"Sometimes when I am alone in my room in the dark, I practice smiling to myself. I do this to be kind to myself, to take good care of myself, to love myself. I know that if I cannot take care of myself, I cannot take care of anyone else."

Be Free Where You Are
Thich Nhat Hanh

THOUGHT FOR THE DAY

Smiling to yourself creates the beginning of calmness within, a little bit of relaxation even among the chaos.

REFLECTION

We've all heard it said that it takes more facial muscles to frown or scowl than it takes to smile. We've all seen the "furrowed brow," on ourselves and on others. If stress can have such an outward effect on the muscles we can see, imagine the effect it might be having on our internal organs! I find that I am more able to stay calm and relaxed if I am mindful of my facial muscles and smile to my self mentally.

- 25 -

"What does music teach us? Music helps us to train ourselves in some way or other in harmony, and it is this which is magic, or the secret behind music. When you hear music that you enjoy, it tunes you and puts you in harmony with life."

The Mysticism of Sound and Music:
The Sufi Teaching of Hazrat Inayat Khan
Shambhala Publications, Inc.

THOUGHT FOR THE DAY

Children seem to know this instinctively—did you ever watch how they swing and sway to any music they hear? Spend some time today sitting still and listening, really listening to some music. Pay close attention to the blending of sounds, and for a while let your self become lost in them.

25

REFLECTION

Not to take anything away from gifted voices, but I find listening to instrumentals a wonderfully relaxing experience, a beautiful blend of piano, violins, cello and saxophone. As I sit here typing, I listen to the music of Mother Nature, the leaves rustling in the wind as a summer storm begins to brew, the sounds of the birds calling to each other as they fly from tree to tree. There is a calming effect in soothing music, whether it's created by instruments or nature.

- 26 -

"The river of life sometimes takes a winding course toward your goal. It may even seem temporarily to be going in a different direction entirely, yet in the long run it is a more effortless and harmonious way to get there than through struggling and striving."

Creative Visualization
Shakti Gawain

THOUGHT FOR THE DAY

So often when a crisis comes up, we need to put off working toward a goal so that we can become a caregiver to a loved one. We need to remember that putting something off for a while does not necessarily mean abandoning it forever. We need to remember that being a caregiver is a gift to our loved one, and that we will reap the rewards over time when we once again begin working toward our personal goal.

- *26* -

REFLECTION

We have been caregivers together for our parents, and separately for other family members. We learned first hand that during the time you spend giving care to another, there are many activities you will have to drop from your daily life, and some of these may include coming close to achieving a long awaited goal. Never become discouraged when something has to be postponed, but rather embrace the opportunity to care for your loved one. Your goal will materialize in due time, and you will be even more able to work toward it knowing that you did your best to make your loved one comfortable, within, of course, your human limitations.

"If you keep compassion alive in you while listening, then anger and irritation cannot arise. Otherwise the things he says, the things she says, will touch off your irritation, anger and suffering. Compassion alone can protect you from becoming irritated, angry, or full of despair."

Anger: Wisdom for Cooling the Flames
Thich Nhat Hanh

THOUGHT FOR THE DAY

Practice having compassion rather than taking someone's comments or behavior personally.

- 27 -

REFLECTION

A professor in one of my undergraduate classes made a statement that I hope I remember for the rest of my life: "When someone does or says something that offends you, stop to think what might be going on in that person's life." I have not always been successful in practicing this, but it has given me a wonderful goal to work toward. During the times I have been able to step back and think of the other person and not only of myself, I have been able to realize that some event had taken place to cause some sadness, anger or hurt feelings in that person. I just happened to be in the wrong place at the wrong time.

- 28 -

"We can begin to relax by just becoming aware of whatever feelings we are experiencing—the tightness in our muscles, difficulties in breathing, or pressure in our heads. We need to be aware of, touch, and communicate with all the feelings that we experience in our daily lives."

Gesture of Balance:
A Guide to Awareness, Self-Healing, and Meditation
Tarthang Tulku

THOUGHT FOR THE DAY

Practicing mindfulness is a way to help me stay focused on what is going on at the moment. If I learn to stay in the moment, I will learn not to worry about the future.

- 28 -

REFLECTION

Worrying about the unknowns that may lie ahead in the future only makes me tense and irritable today. When I take the time to plan for the future, then let it go and take one step at a time, I find that I am more relaxed and able to function more effectively, even in stressful situations.

- 29 -

"Grief is the conflicting group of human emotions caused by an end to or change in a familiar pattern."

The Grief Recovery Handbook
John W. James and Russell Friedman

THOUGHT FOR THE DAY

While grief is most often associated with the death of a loved one, it can also be the result of anything from having a good friend move out of the neighborhood to the death of a pet. Grief is often a part of a caregiver's range of emotions because we come face to face with the likelihood that our loved one's life is changed forever, and all we can do is our best to make the transitions easier.

REFLECTION

Most people associate the word "grief" with the death of a loved one, but grief happens with any type of life changing loss. Rose and Juanita have experienced most of the losses that, unfortunately, happen to the average person: the uncertainty that follows a divorce; the physical restrictions that come with arthritis, carpal tunnel, and knee pain from a torn meniscus; the illness and death of a loved pet. The loss of a parent is something we all will experience at one time or another during our lives; it almost seems to be the natural order of things. The sudden death of Juanita's son by suicide in 1995 at the age of 28, and the brutal murder of Rose and Juanita's sister in 2004, however, are losses that left the entire family not only grieving but looking for answers and wondering "why?" We have to be careful not to put a time limit on our or anyone's grief.

- *30* -

"We are close again, or maybe for the first time, because now we choose to be. The threat of everlasting separation has united us as it did thirty-two years ago when our mother died. But this time no one is shrugging it off or too young to remember This time no one can deny its impact on all of us."

An Arrow Through The Heart
Deborah Daw Heffernan

THOUGHT FOR THE DAY

Help me to appreciate each person I meet today. Help me to be aware of the fragility of life on a daily basis.

- 30 -

REFLECTION

We have all had experiences that brought us face to face with the reality of the fragility of life. A child dies suddenly. Someone leaves for work in the morning and never comes home. Unfortunately, the stark realization that helps us appreciate our loved ones often leaves us after the shock wears off, and we go back to responding to the people in our lives with the same intolerance, impatience, and criticism as before. This has happened to me more often than I want to remember. Danny's and Carol's unexpected and sudden deaths remind us to show compassion and respect to everyone, every day, and, above all, to never be shy about saying "I love you."

- *31* -

"Maintain a sense of humor; it will get you through many crises. The sick person is still a person. He needs and enjoys a good laugh too."

The 36-Hour Day
Nancy L. Mace, M.A.
Peter V. Rabins, M.D., M.P.H

THOUGHT FOR THE DAY

Help me not to take myself or life too seriously,
and to learn to wear the world like a loose garment.
Help me to notice and share the little things in life
that make me smile.

- *31* -

REFLECTION

When it comes to keeping a sense of humor, Dad was such a good example! Anyone in our large extended family could relate instances of when Dad would break up a stressful situation with a little bit of humor, and yet without being disrespectful to the gravity of the situation.

AFTERWORD

We would strongly urge those with aging parents to spend more than daytime hours with them. We visited our parents often, sometimes coming in the late morning and staying until evening. But we had no idea of the gravity of Mom's condition because Dad did all he could do to cover for her. We saw that Mom did not cook anymore, but Dad insisted it was that he no longer felt like eating big meals. After all, he said, the older you get, the less it takes to get you going! Also, Mom and Dad, who were always conscious of the environment, started using only disposable cups, plates, and dinnerware. Dad said it was his idea so that Mom did not have so much work to do. We didn't realize how serious the situation was until we starting staying overnight when Dad got sick. If we had noticed patterns of behavior sooner, perhaps Mom would have been put on Aracept sooner, and perhaps we could have shared Dad's burden instead of him having to be Mom's sole caregiver. A few days before he passed away, Dad sat in his rocker, put his head into his hands and cried. I knelt at his knee and listened as he asked "Who is going to take care of my wife?" I told him that no one could ever take his place, but that Rose and I would do our best to care for Mom the way he would want us to. Dad looked me in the eye and quietly sobbed, "You don't understand. Who is going to take care of her?" At the time, we did not know that he was referring to the behavior that would be diagnosed as Alzheimer's.

We hope that something in this little book will help you make good decisions in the care of your loved ones, and to understand that the most important decision you will make is to take good care of your self.

Rose is a certified massage therapist, with a background in oncology massage. She is also a certified infant massage instructor. Rose is currently volunteering at Rush University Hospital, Chicago, working with cancer patients at the Cancer Integrative Medicine Program.

Juanita received a B.S. in applied psychology from Loyola University Chicago, and an M.A. in pastoral studies from the Institute of Pastoral Studies/Loyola University Chicago. She is a Grief ♣ Recovery® Specialist and received training from The Grief Recovery Institute®. Juanita has created a series of workshops based on the practice of mindfulness and spiritual growth.

Rose can be reached at
rxk51@hotmail.com

Juanita can be reached at
jliepelt@sbcglobal.net

WORKS CITED

A Passion for the Possible. Jean Houston. New York, New York: HarperCollins, 1997.

All Our Losses, All Our Griefs. Kenneth R. Mitchell and Herbert Anderson. Philadelphia, Pennsylvania: The Westminster Press, 1983.

An Arrow Through the Heart. Deborah Daw Heffernan. New York, New York: The Free Press, a Division of Simon & Schuster, Inc.

Anger: Wisdom for Cooling the Flames. Thich Nhat Hanh. New York, New York: Riverhead Books, published by The Berkley Publishing Group, A Division of Penguin Putnam Inc., 2001.

Awakening The Buddha Within: Tibetan Wisdom for the Western World. Lama Surya Das. New York, New York: Bantam Doubleday Dell Publishing Group, Inc., 1997.

Be Free Where You Are. Thich Nhat Hanh. Berkeley, California: Parallax Press, 2002.

Creative Visualization. Shakti Gawain. Novato, California: Nataraj Publishing, A Division of New World Library, 2002, 1995, 1978.

Gesture of Balance: A Guide to Awareness, Self-healing, and Meditation. Tarthang Tulku. Berkeley, California: Dharma Publishing, 1977.

Guilt is the Teacher, Love is the Lesson. Joan Borysenko, Ph.D. New York, New York: Warner Books, Inc., 1990.

Healing Words: The Power of Prayer and the Practice of Medicine. Larry Dossey, M.D. New York: HarperCollins, 1993.

Inspiration, Your Ultimate Calling. Dr. Wayne W. Dyer. Carlsbad, California; London; Sydney; Johannesburg; Vancouver; Hong Kong; Mumbai. Hay House, 2006.

Peace is Every Step: The Path of Mindfulness in Everyday Life. Thich Nhat Hanh. New York, New York: Bantam Books, a Division of Bantam Doubleday Dell Publishing Group, Inc. 1991.

The 36-Hour Day. Nancy L. Mace, M.A., and Peter V. Rabins, M.D., M.P.H. New York, New York and Boston, Massachusetts: Warner Books, 1981, 1991, 1999.

The Creation of Health: The Emotional, Psychological and Spiritual Responses That Promote Health and Healing. Caroline Myss, Ph.D. and C. Norman Shealy, M.D., Ph.D. New York, New York: Three Rivers Press, A Division of Crown Publishers, Inc., 1988, 1993.

The Feeling Buddha: A Buddhist Psychology of Character, Adversity and Passion. David Brazier. New York, New York: PALGRAVE, 1997.

The Grief Recovery Handbook. John W. James and Russell Friedman. New York, New York: HarperCollins Publishers, 1998.

The Healer's Calling: A Spirituality for Physicians and Other Health Care Professionals. Daniel P. Sulmasy, O.F.M., M.D. New York, New York and Mahwah, New Jersey: Paulist Press, 1997.

The Mysticism of Sound and Music: The Sufi Teaching of Hazrat Inayat Khan. Shambhala Publications, Inc., 1991.

The Power of Now. Eckhart Tolle. Novato, California: New World Library, 1999.

The Way of St. Francis: The Challenge of Franciscan Spirituality for Everyone. Murray Bodo, O.F.M., Garden City, New York: Image Books, a Division of Doubleday & Company, Inc., 1984.

Unconditional Life: Mastering the Forces that Shape Personal Reality. Deepak Chopra, M.D. Bantam Books, 1991.

Why People Don't Heal and How They Can. Caroline Myss, Ph.D. New York, New York: Three Rivers Press, A Division of Crown Publishers, Inc., 2001.

ADDENDUM

The practice of mindfulness is nothing more than maintaining an awareness of the present moment—not judging anything or anyone—not agreeing or disagreeing with anyone or any situation—simply being aware of the fact that what is *is*. Practicing mindfulness teaches us to pay attention to each moment, and to each action that is being performed and each word that is said in that moment.

As we progress in our practice of mindfulness, we learn to value each moment because life's circumstances are constantly changing. When we look at the big picture, we come to realize that when we make the most of each moment, we actually have more control over our future. The benefits of mindfulness range from developing a more stress-free and healthy lifestyle to being more productive on the job.

Christopher Chroniak, Ph.D., is a licensed clinical psychologist and the founder and director of The Insight Center where he is a teacher of mindfulness meditation. Rose and Juanita had their first hands-on experience of the benefits of mindfulness after taking the course taught by Dr. Chroniak, "Mindfulness-Based Stress Reduction." This course is based on the program developed by Jon Kabat-Zinn, Ph.D., and discussed in detail in his book *Full Catastrophe Living: Using the Wisdom of Your Body and Mind to Face Stress, Pain, and Illness.* This is the program of the Stress Reduction Clinic at the University of Massachusetts Medical Center.

RECOMMENDED READING

Awakening to the Sacred: Creating a Personal Spiritual Life.
Lama Surya Das. Broadway Books, 1999.

Wherever You Go, There You Are. Jon Kabat-Zinn, Ph.D.
Hyperion, 1994.

*Full Castrophe Living: Using the Wisdom of Your Body and
Mind to Face Stress, Pain, and Illness.* Jon Kabat-Zinn, Ph.D.
Dell Publishing, 1990.

The Miracle of Mindfulness. Thich Nhat Hahn. Beacon
Press, 1975, 1976.

Be Here Now. Ram Dass. 1971.

RECOMMENDED WEB SITES TO VISIT

www.theinsightcenter.com

www.mettamassagetherapy.com

WORTH REMEMBERING

"Constant awareness of whatever we are doing is even more important than formal meditation or practice, for when we are mindful every moment, our confidence and balance increase. And eventually we will understand how crucial every thought, word, and action is, both for ourselves and for others."

Gesture of Balance: A Guide to Awareness, Self-Healing, and Meditation
Tarthang Tulku

"There is no reason why mindfulness should be different from focusing all one's attention on one's work, to be alert and to be using one's best judgment. During the moment one is consulting, resolving, and dealing with whatever arises, a calm heart and self-control are necessary if one is to obtain good results."

The Miracle of Mindfulness
Thich Nhat Hanh

Printed in the United States
86824LV00001B/130-177/A

9 780979 131745